How to be Mother's helper

by Camille Sokol
pictures by Bill Sokol

How
to be
Mother's
helper

by Camille Sokol

pictures by Bill Sokol

Platt & Munk, Publishers / New York

Contents

Do you ever wish you could

prepare food that tastes as good as your mother's? Here are several delicious recipes for you to fix yourself.

Have you ever wondered how the yarn in your sweater stays together? In this book you will learn the secrets of knitting, and at the same time you'll be making useful things.

This brimful book of ideas will make you love doing nice things around the house. You'll find out how to start a lemon tree with just one seed. You'll see what you can do with bright scraps of paper besides throw them away.

Now, turn the page and start right in—and have fun!

1. Learning to knit

All you need are knitting needles and heavy wool or cotton yarn, and there are all sorts of things you can knit. Keep all your knitting things together in a small bag or basket.

Napkin ring

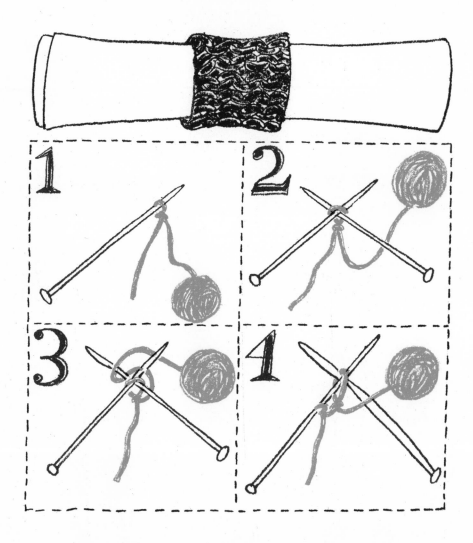

First, cast on 6 stitches. Tie a knot around your needle. Put your needle through the loop. Carry the yarn around the needle. Slip it onto the needle.

Now you have 2 stitches. Put your needle through the second loop. Carry the yarn around the needle. Bring the loop through under the needle. Make 6 stitches.

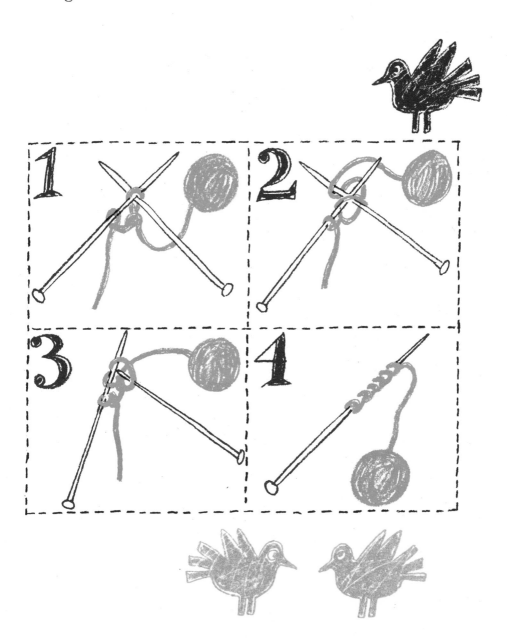

14 Now you begin to knit. Put your needle through the first loop. Carry the yarn around the needle. Bring the loop through under the needle. Now slide off the loop onto the next needle. Keep the yarn outside.

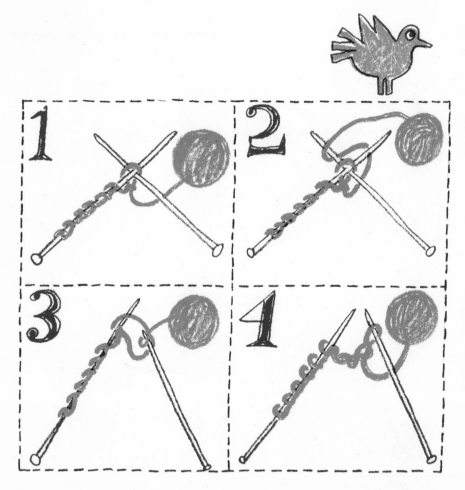

Do a second stitch.
Put your needle through the next loop.
Carry the yarn around.
Bring the loop through under the needle.
Always keep the yarn outside.
Now you have knitted 2 stitches.
Knit the 6 stitches.

Turn your needle and begin a second row.
Keep the yarn outside.

When the band measures about 5 inches, cast off.

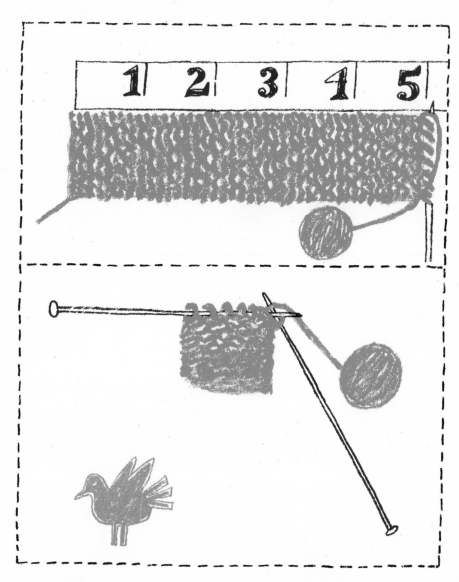

Put your needle through the first loop.
Carry the yarn around.
Bring the loop through under the needle.
Slide it off.

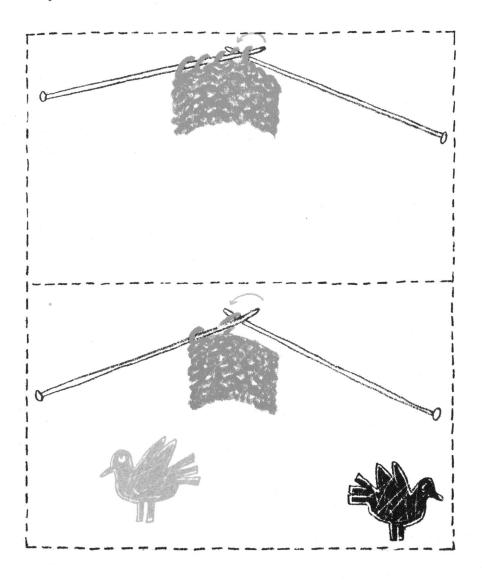

Do a second stitch.
Now you have 2 stitches on one needle.
With your needle carry the first one over the second one.
Knit another stitch.
Carry the first one over the second one.
Do this until you have done all the stitches, and you have
only 1 stitch left.

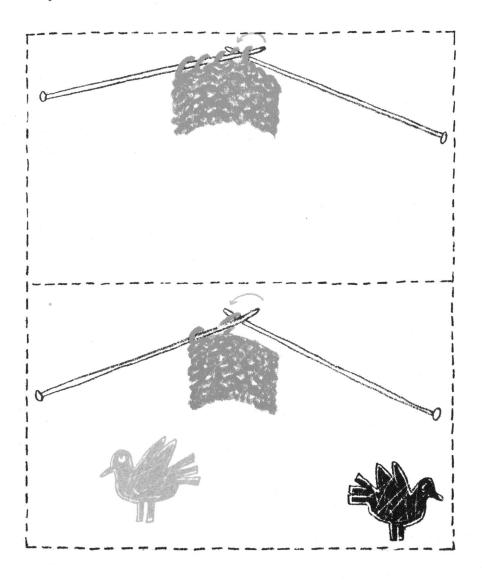

Cut the yarn about 12 inches away from the needle.
Pass the yarn through the loop. Pull it tight.

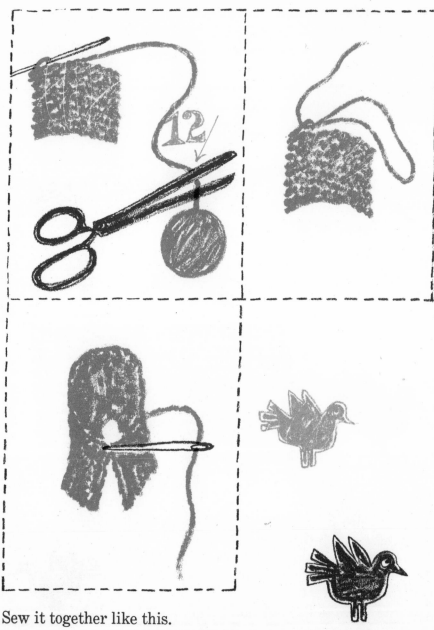

Sew it together like this.

Coaster

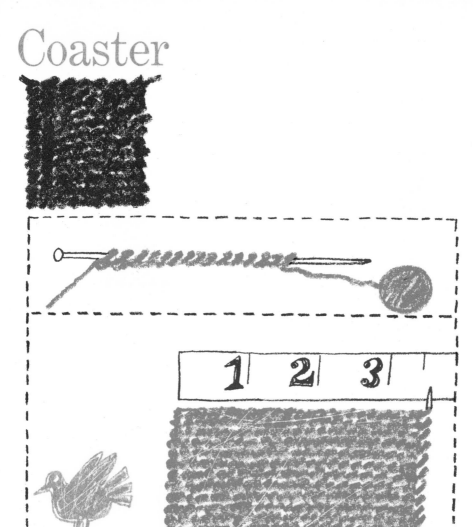

Cast on 15 stitches.
Look on page 12 for the directions on how to cast on.
Then knit a square until it measures 3½ inches.
Cast off.
Look on page 16 for the directions on how to cast off.
Cut the ends off.
Pat into place with your hand.

Potholder

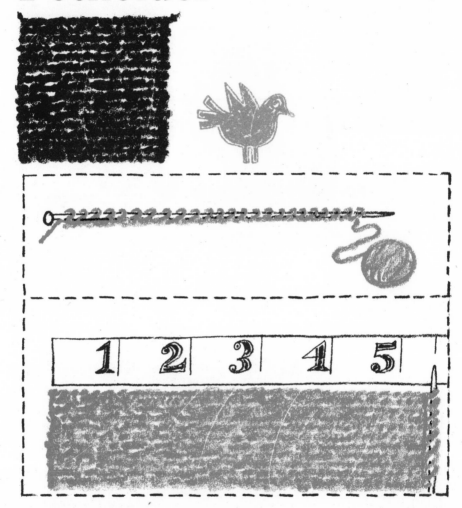

Cast on 24 stitches.
If you have forgotten how, look on page 12.
Knit until the potholder measures about 5½ inches.
Then cast off.
Look on page 16 for the directions.
Cut the ends off.
Pat into place with your hand.

Hair band

Cast on 12 stitches.
Knit until the band is 18½ inches long.

Cast off. Sew it together like this.

Doll scarf

Cast on 4 stitches.
Knit until the small band measures 8½ inches.
Cast off as on page 16.
Cut the ends off.
Pat into place.

You could make one in blue or red or yellow.

If you follow these basic directions you will be able to think of many other things to knit. For instance, you can knit lots of small squares and sew them together to make a doll blanket.

2. How to make table mats

If you'd like to make the table look prettier in the dining room or in the kitchen, you can make table mats with napkins to match. Here are several ways to make them. Keep your materials together. A shoebox is perfect for paints, scissors, brushes and your sewing things.

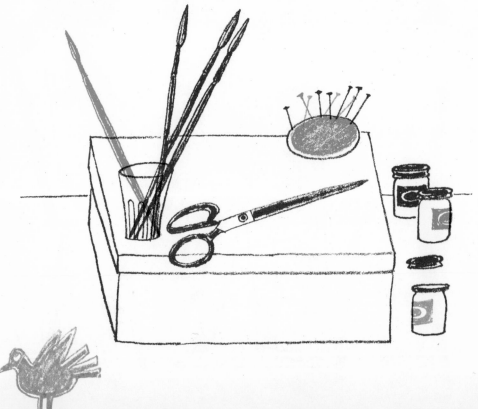

Raveling

Cut 4 pieces of cloth.
You need cloth that can easily ravel, like burlap or heavy
woven cotton, 19 inches long and 13 inches wide.

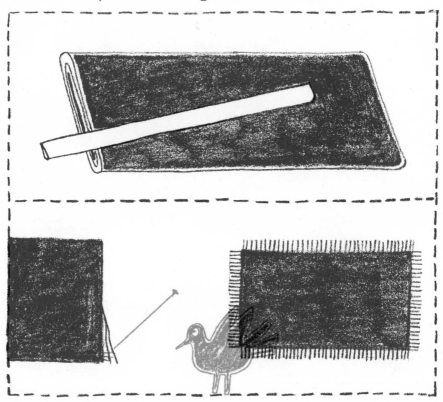

With a pin, pull the thread out like this.

Do it for about 1 inch.

Pull the threads on one side, then on the other side.

Do all 4 sides.

Press flat.

Napkins to match.

If you use burlap for your table mats, use heavy
cotton for the napkins.

Cut 4 pieces, 12 inches long and 12 inches wide.
Pull the threads on one side, then on the other side.
Do all 4 sides.
Press flat.

Fold in half. Then in half again.

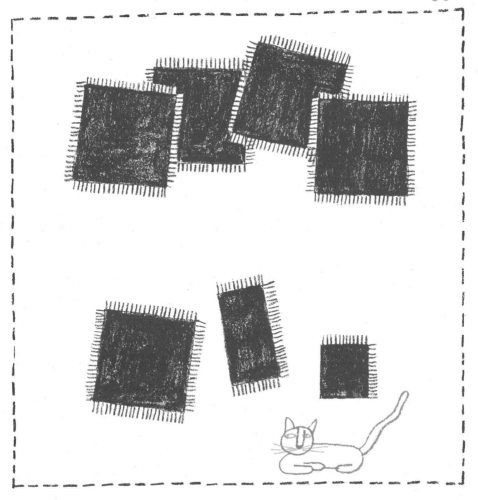

Embroidering

Cut 4 pieces of cloth, 19 inches long and 13 inches wide.
Thread a heavy needle with colored floss.
Make it a different color from the mat.
Tie a knot in the floss.

Begin at the bottom corner like this.

Hold the floss down with your thumb.
Push your needle on top of the floss.
Pull your needle through.
Move about ¼ inch away.
Hold the floss down with your thumb.
Push your needle on top of the floss.
Pull your needle through.

30   Go around the mat.
When you get to the knot, go in and out three times.
Cut the floss.
Press it.

Napkins to match.

Cut 4 pieces of cloth, 12 inches long and 12 inches wide.
See page 28 and do the same.

Stenciling

Cut 4 pieces of paper, 19 inches long and 13 inches wide.
Put some poster paint on a piece of wax paper.
Slice a carrot in half and use the top part, or use
a cork top from a bottle.

Dab the cork or carrot in the paint.

32 Press circles in the top left corner.
Add lines with a brush.
Do the same in the bottom right corner.

Napkins to match.

Use plain paper napkins.

Do 4 in the same design.

More stenciling

Cut 4 pieces of wax paper, 5 inches long and 5 inches wide.
Fold them in half.

Draw the half shape of a diamond, or a heart,
or a club or a spade.
Like this.

Now cut it out.
Open it, and place it at the top so that the edges will match.

With a stiff brush, dab on the poster paint.
Move the stencil to the next corner and do the same.
Put one in each corner.

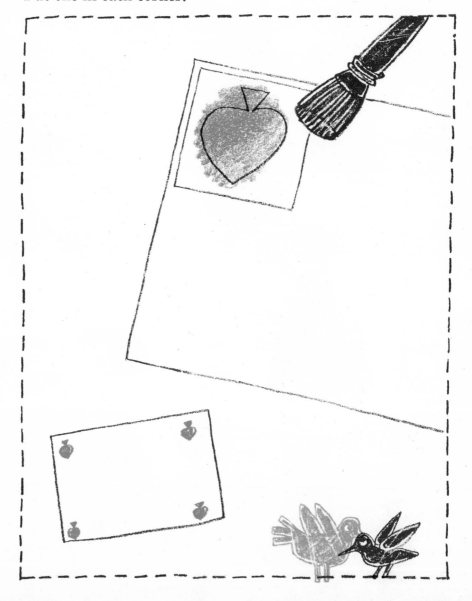

Napkins to match.

Use plain paper napkins.
Dab just one design in the center.

The paper mats and napkins will probably have to be thrown
away after they're used, but you can make new
ones the same way with your own designs.

3. Fun in the kitchen

Whether you feel like having a party or you are just plain hungry, there are delicious things you can make. Always wash the dishes when you finish and put everything back where it was.

Cheese spread

4 or 5 scallions, chopped fine.
1 package of cream cheese (large size).
¼ teaspoon of salt.
Mix together in a large bowl.
Spread it on some crackers,
or spread it on some bread
and then cut it into different shapes.

Fruit cup

This could be your own special kind of fruit cup,
because you can substitute anything you like.

Slice 1 banana in a large bowl.
Peel and cut 1 apple into slices.
Peel 1 orange and section it.
A few grapes.
1 small can of diced pineapple, and the juice.
1 teaspoon of sugar.
½ cup of water.
Mix it all together.

Sandwiches

Butter 2 slices of bread.
Spread your bread with any of these:
Cream cheese.
Peanut butter.
Your favorite jelly.
If you have any cold cuts, you could put on a slice of
ham and a slice of cheese.
Or a slice of cheese and some slices of tomato.
You could make a favorite of mine:
Toast 2 slices of white bread.
Butter the toast.
Slice 1 banana on the toast.

Salad

1 can of tuna fish.
1 small onion, chopped fine.
3 or 4 stalks of celery, chopped.
½ teaspoon of oil and ½ teaspoon of vinegar.
½ teaspoon of salt.
Mix all together in a large bowl.
Slice some green pepper, or slice some radishes,
and decorate the platter, like this.

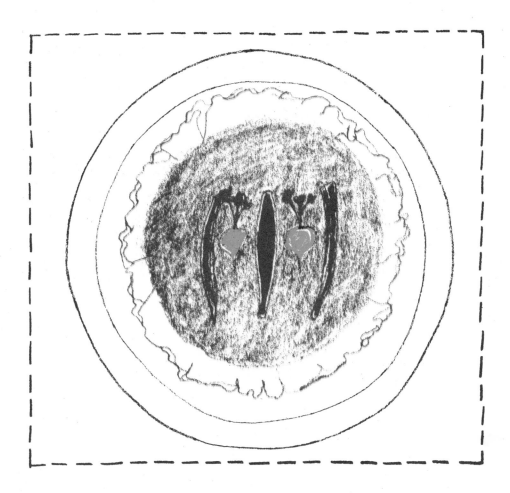

Flavored milk

Strawberry milk:
1 glass of milk.
1 tablespoon of strawberry syrup
(the kind you make soda with).

Chocolate milk:
1 glass of milk.
1 tablespoon of chocolate syrup.

Vanilla milk:
1 glass of milk.
½ teaspoon of vanilla flavoring.
1 teaspoon of sugar.

You'll be able to think of other wonderful snacks
to fix if you remember these basic directions.

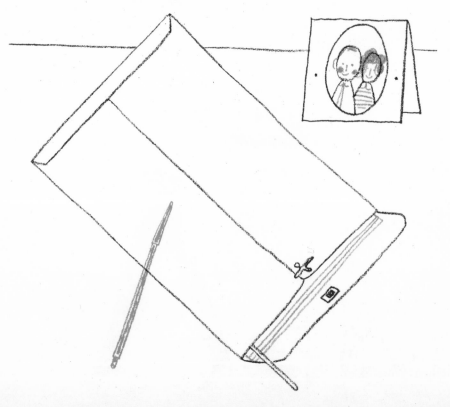

4. How to write letters

If you are away from home, and you want to say "hello" to someone who's still there, or if you are at home and you feel lonesome, you can write a letter. It's a good idea always to keep your paper in a box or large envelope so it won't get dirty. Keep your pen inside, too.

On a sheet of paper, write with a ballpoint pen.
Like this:

Your Address
Your City, State and Zip Code
The Date

Dear Mom and Dad,
    I forgot to give you Sport's ball. It's under my bed.
    If Johnny comes over while I'm gone, tell him he can play with Sport.
    I went to the baseball game yesterday with Uncle Cy. We had lots of fun. See you soon.

                    Your Name

Sign your name

Or if you would like some information:

Your Address
Your City, state and Zip Code
The Date

Chamber of Commerce
The Address
The City, state and Zip Code

Dear Sir:
   My family and I are planning to visit your state this summer.
   I would like some information on places of interest to visit. Thank you.

Yours truly,
Your Name

Address your letter like this:

Your Name
Your Address
Your City and state
Zip Code

The Person's Name
The Person's Address
The City and state
Zip Code

Put a stamp on your letter.
Now you can mail it and wait for an answer.

5. Growing a garden

Put some soil in a pot, or a small can or jar or a paper cup. Now you're ready to start your own plant. Don't forget that plants need light and water.

Sunflower seed

If it's a flower you would like, you could use a sunflower seed.

Press the sunflower seed with a pencil,
½ inch into the soil.
Like this.
Water it every day. Then watch it grow.

Watermelon seed

If it's a vine you would like, you could use a watermelon seed.

Press the watermelon seed with a pencil,
½ inch into the soil.
Water it every day.

Lemon or grapefruit pit

If it's a small tree you want, you could use a lemon or grapefruit pit.

Press the lemon or grapefruit pit with a pencil, ½ inch into the soil.
Water it every day.

Avocado pit

If you would like a big tall tree, you could use an
avocado pit. Cut the avocado in ½ like this.

Carefully remove the pit.
In a small dish, put the flat part of the pit at
the bottom. Now, fill it with water halfway.
Leave the top part out like this.

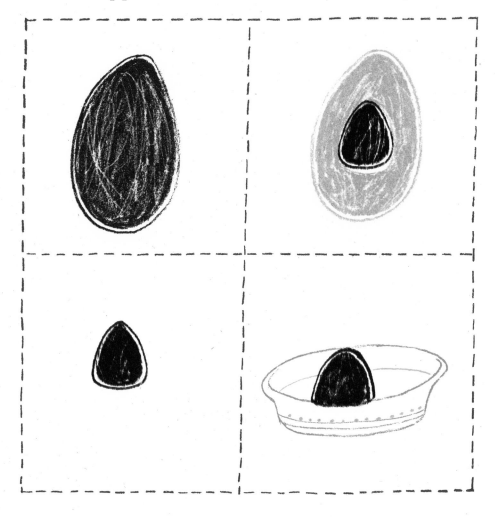

Add water every day to keep the water level halfway.
Roots will form at the bottom.
When the stalk is about 8 inches tall,
you can transplant it:

Fill a big pot with some soil.
Now dig out a handful the size of the pit.
Gently put the pit into the hole.
Now put the soil back in.
Press the soil tightly around the pit.
Leave the top uncovered.

Don't forget to water it every day.

When your plants have grown too big for their pots
you can transplant them.

Go carefully around the edge of the pot with a knife.
Like this.
The plant will come out easily.
Get a bigger pot.
Fill it with soil.
Take out a handful, the size of the roots of the plant.

Now put the plant in.
Press the soil around it tightly with your thumb.
Like this.
Water it every day.

Follow all these directions carefully and you might be
as lucky as Jack was with his beanstalk!

6. Fun with paper

A little imagination, some scissors, a few bits of paper, some paste, and you can be creative. In case you spill some paint, it's best to spread out newspaper first.

Mobile

Cut some shapes out of construction paper like this.
You can trace these with a piece of wax paper.
Draw the outline.
Now trace them back on to the construction paper.
Or, if you like, you can use cookie cutters,
or make your own shapes.

Now cut 1 piece of paper 10 inches long and 1½ inches wide.
And 2 pieces 8 inches long and 1½ inches wide.
Cut 5 pieces of black thread 12 inches long.
And 2 pieces 10 inches long.
With a needle, punch holes here.
Now tie the shapes like this.

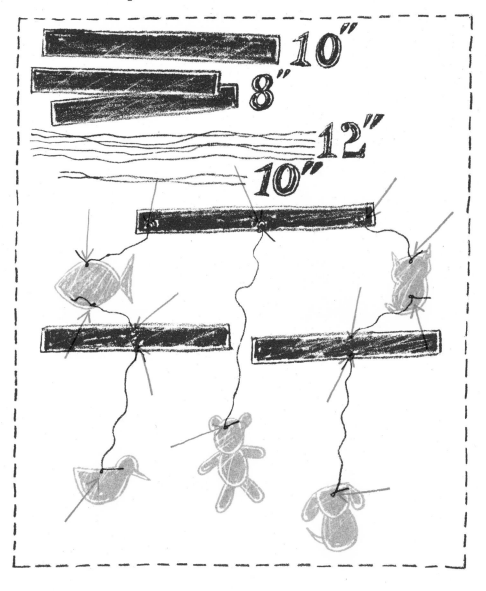

Collage

Maybe you would like something to hang on your wall.
Take a piece of cardboard,
and small pieces of cloth, or small pieces of
paper, or anything that you can glue.

Cut these small pieces into shapes that you like.
Now glue them on to the cardboard to form a bird,
a fish or a bowl of fruit.
You could color some of the shapes with poster paint.

Necklace or bracelet

Cut some squares,
and some circles,
and thread them together
to make a necklace or a bracelet.

Take a dime, a nickle, a penny and a quarter.
Draw around these to make different-sized circles.
Or make straight lines across the paper.
Now make the lines go from top to bottom.
Cut the shapes.

Thread a mending needle with some string
long enough to fit over your head.
Now just push the shapes on to the needle.

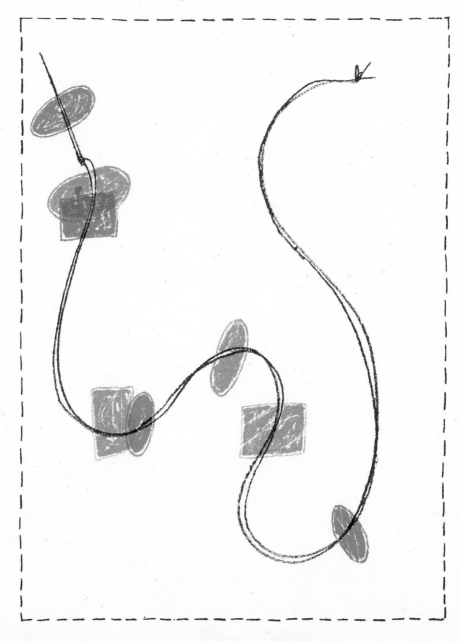

When it's long enough to make a necklace,
cut the string.
Tie the string together.
Do the same for a bracelet.

Now you can make something out of paper
for everyone in your family!